Married Life

Married Life

An Inside Look

Andrew P. Manion and Amy Schlumpf Manion

Saint Mary's Press
Christian Brothers Publications
Winona, Minnesota

Genuine recycled paper with 10% post-consumer waste.
Printed with soy-based ink.

The publishing team included Shirley Kelter, development editor; Paul Grass, FSC, copy editor; Brooke Saron, production editor; Hollace Storkel, typesetter; Laurie Geisler, art director; cover and inside image copyright © Digital Vision/PictureQuest; manufactured by the production services department of Saint Mary's Press.

The acknowledgments continue on page 77.

Printed in the United States of America.

Printing: 9 8 7 6 5 4 3 2 1

Year: 2009 08 07 06 05 04 03 02 01

ISBN 0-88489-722-2

Library of Congress Cataloging-in-Publication Data

Manion, Andrew P.
    Married life: an inside look / Andrew P. Manion and Amy Schlumpf Manion.
        p. cm.
    ISBN 0-88489-722-2 (pbk.)
        1. Marriage—Religious aspects—Catholic Church. 2. Catholic Church—Doctrines. I. Manion, Amy Schlumpf. II. Title.
    BX2250 .M255 2001
    248.8'44'08822—dc21
                                                            2001000976

*We lovingly dedicate this book
to the four people who have taught us
virtually everything we know
about living our marriage vows
without ever interfering in our marriage:
our parents,
Thomas A. and Maureen O. Manion,
and
Edward E. and Mary W. Schlumpf.*

Contents

Series Foreword

An old Hasidic legend about the mysterious nature of life says that God whispers into your newly created soul all the secrets of your existence, all the divine love for you, and your unique purpose in life. Then, just as God infuses your soul into your body, an assisting angel presses your mouth shut and instructs your soul to forget its preternatural life.

You are now spending your time on earth seeking to know once again the God who created you, loves you, and assigns you a singular purpose. Raise your forefinger to feel the crease mark the angel left above your lips, and ask yourself in wonder: "Who am I? How am I uniquely called to live in the world?"

The authors of the five titles in this Vocations series tell how they approached these same questions as they searched for meaning and purpose in their Christian vocation, whether as a brother, a married couple, a priest, a single person, or a sister.

Christians believe that God creates a dream for each person. What is your dream in life? This is how Pope John Paul II, echoing Jeremiah 1:5, speaks of the Creator's dream and the divine origin of your vocation:

All human beings, from their mothers' womb, belong to God who searches them and knows them, who forms them and knits them together with his own hands, who gazes on them when they are tiny shapeless embryos and already sees in them the adults of tomorrow whose days are numbered and whose vocation is even now written in the "book of life." (*Evangelium Vitae*, no. 61)

In spite of believing that God does have your specific vocation in mind, you probably share the common human experience—the tension and the mystery—of finding out who you are and how God is personally calling you to live in this world. Although you can quickly recognize the uniqueness of your thumbprint, you will spend a lifetime deciphering the full meaning of your originality.

There is no shortage of psychological questionnaires for identifying your personality type, career path, learning style, and even a compatible mate. Although these methods can be helpful in your journey to self-discovery, they do little to illuminate the mystery in your quest. What is the best approach to knowing your vocation in life? Follow the pathway as it unfolds before you and live with the questions that arise along the way.

The stories in this Vocations series tell about life on the path of discernment and choice; they remind you that you are not alone. God is your most present and patient companion. In the "travelogues" of these authors, you will find reassurance that even when you relegate the Divine Guide to keeping ten paces behind you, or when you abandon the path entirely for a time, you cannot undo God's faithfulness to you. Each vocation story uniquely testifies to the truth that God is always at work revealing your life's purpose to you.

In these stories you will also find that other traveling companions—family, friends, and classmates—contribute to your discovery of a place in the world and call forth the person you are becoming. Their companionship along the way not only manifests God's abiding presence but also reminds you to respect others for their gifts, which highlight and mirror your own.

Although each path in the Vocations series is as unique as the person who tells his or her story, these accounts remind you to be patient with the mystery of your own life, to have confidence in God's direction, and to listen to the people and events you encounter as you journey to discover your unique role in God's plan. By following your path, you too will come to see the person of tomorrow who lives in you today.

Clare vanBrandwijk

Introduction

A Marriage, Not Just a Wedding

When we told our parents that we had been asked to write a book about Catholic marriage, their reaction was pretty much what you would expect from the people who had raised us and taught us by their example most of what we know about being Catholic and being married: they laughed. It wasn't a mean laugh; we think they were just amused at the idea that a couple with a mere dozen years of experience with this thing called marriage might be ready to impart advice on the topic. The experience of our parents notwithstanding, we took comfort in the knowledge that this book would be aimed primarily at young people—for whom twelve years sounds like more than half a lifetime (and rightly so).

We do not claim to be experts on the subject, other than that we have some experience (twelve years each with marriage, thirty-some with Catholicism). We are not marriage counselors, although we have helped and counseled couples preparing for marriage. We are not psychologists (actually one of us is, but not the kind that specializes in marriage issues). We are not theologians who know the intricacies of Catholic church doctrine on the sacrament of marriage, although we think we know the basics.

What we are is a couple trying to live our wedding vows every day. By sharing our experiences with young people, we hope to help them prepare for what lies ahead, whether they consider marriage as a vague concept in the distant future (like parenthood, mutual funds, and retirement) or have already set the date for the ceremony.

Before looking at a marriage that lies ahead, however, perhaps you ought to determine *whether* married life is for you. Although the majority of people in our culture do get married, a significant minority do not. After careful discernment, some people determine that their call is to enter religious life. Others discern that neither married life nor religious life is right for them.

The mistake that many people make, to the constant annoyance of those who are single, is to assume that all unmarried people wish they were married—and would be if they found "the right person." For many happily single people, the right person is themselves. Most of the single people we know have larger circles of friends, spend more time with them, and are able to devote more of their energy to causes such as social justice than the married people we know. They tend to give of themselves in ways that married people often cannot. Although single people at one time or another may envy the emotional intimacy that married couples share, married people sometimes may resent the balance of sociability and solitude that singles enjoy.

We suggest another thing to note about this book: it is not intended to convince you that you ought to get married. Although we love our marriage, we know that marriage is not for everyone. This book will help you determine whether married life is right for you.

A wedding is an event;
a marriage is a process.

The title of this introduction highlights the distinction between a wedding and a marriage: a wedding is an event; a marriage is a process. Traditionally, a wedding is when friends and family gather to celebrate as the couple pledge their love for each other, before those present and before God, and mark the beginning of their life together. It is a sacred event and a fun one, to be sure; Jesus performed his first public miracle at a wedding, and he did it so that those celebrating the sacred event could continue to have fun.

Some weddings are more private than others; some couples elope. Whether a wedding is shared by four people or four hundred, it is a commencement of sorts. A new life begins. The vows that the couple take do more than fill the time between "We are gathered here today" and "You may now kiss the bride." In reciting these vows, the woman and the man promise to each other, to their families and friends, and to God that they will be together for the rest of their life. They acknowledge that with this promise they are becoming something different than what they were before. They were two lives, but now they are one. Even our language recognizes the uniqueness of this relationship: "They begin their life together," rather than the more grammatically sensible, "They begin their lives together." It is this life that we will focus on in this book: the marriage, the lifelong process that happens after the guests have gone home, the pictures are in the album, and the credit card bill from the honeymoon is due.

The Wedding Industry

Popular culture has a lot to say about weddings. There are magazines, such as *Bride's Magazine* and *Modern Bride,* devoted to preparing for the wedding day, including the omnipresent "bride's checklist." There are bridal showers, bridal shops, and even massive bridal expos that gather under one roof providers of gowns, cakes, and music, as well as caterers and travel agencies, to sell their wares and services to couples-to-be. It is also common to see in general magazines for young women articles about weddings, as well as about identifying and attracting a mate.

Notice these two interesting things about the bridal industry: First, it is massive, especially when compared to the relatively small marriage industry, which consists primarily of books about maintaining or restoring a happy marriage, counseling for married couples in trouble, and jewelers happy to sell anniversary rings.

Second, a glance at wedding-related publications, businesses, and services reveals that they are overwhelmingly geared toward brides. There are no *Modern Groom* magazines, groom shops, or "groomal expos," nor is there such a word as *groomal*. Men's magazines, although filled with ideas about how males can make themselves more physically attractive and illustrated with pictures of physically attractive women, contain precious little information about how to identify and attract a wife and even less on how to be a good husband. Given that today's culture promotes marriage among women and discourages it among men, it is no wonder that there is plenty of confusion and miscommunication. When we were younger, we witnessed the worldwide television event of the late Princess Diana's supposed Fairy-tale Wedding. We never heard once about Prince Charles's Fairy-tale Wedding. Wasn't he there, too?

Imagine an archaeologist from another planet who comes to earth sometime in the future and studies the relevant artifacts of today. The alien might have this to say about weddings and marriage in the United States at the turn of the twenty-first century:

Marriage was an institution engaged in by most of the humans of this period. The marriage was preceded by a period of preparation called an engagement, when the female (called the bride) was expected to develop a "checklist." This checklist was a kind of test that had to be completed before the wedding would be allowed to take place. It included items like "select gown," "choose reception site," "pick DJ," "select photographer," "choose cake," "choose bridesmaids' gowns," "borrow something for wedding," "remind groom to identify groomsmen," and "attend expo." I found no evidence that the groom had any such checklist. The wedding was the event wherein the couple promised each other that they would remain married for the rest of their life. A honeymoon often followed that had been arranged at a bridal expo. Details on the actual marriages are not available, other than that about half of them ended considerably earlier than the previously agreed-upon time frame (see Divorce).

Contemporary culture encourages too much wedding preparation and not enough marriage preparation. The result is much unnecessary stress over weddings and a lot of unhappy marriages. Notice that you never hear much about Princess Diana's Fairy-tale *Marriage*; in fact, it seems that it was not a fairy tale at all. Many young couples fail to realize (at the expense of their own happiness) that in the long run it is much more important to agree on how to raise their children, how to deal with relocating to another part of the country, and how to spend their vacation time than it is to negotiate the colors of the bridal party, the china pattern in the gift registry, and the choice of serving beef or chicken at the reception.

If couples spent as much time preparing for marriage as for the wedding, the divorce rate would be lower than it is.

Chances are that if couples spent as much time preparing for marriage as for the wedding, the divorce rate would be lower than it is. We hope that this book makes some small contribution to balancing the scales toward long-term marriage planning.

Fortunately, the Catholic church requires that couples entering the sacrament of marriage attend marriage-preparation meetings, classes, or retreats—often called pre-Cana experiences. (Because Jesus performed his first public miracle at a wedding in Cana, *pre-Cana* means "before the wedding.") We have served as marriage-preparation counselors for our parish, working with couples on an inventory called "Prepare" (by David H. Olsen, David G. Fournier, and John M. Druckman). On this useful tool, the bride- and groom-to-be record their opinions and beliefs about topics like money management, religious practices, child rearing, leisure activities, and career expectations. They compare their opinions with those of their prospective mate, and the counselors work with them on those areas where discrepancies exist. By working through these issues beforehand (with a more experienced pair to guide them), the couple stand a much better chance of dealing effectively with the speed bumps along the road to happiness in their own marriage.

The Wedding Ceremony

Before describing the layout of this book, we would like to get right to the most important part—the ritual of the marriage ceremony, which provides the basis for the book's format.

Although a couple may modify or personalize their marriage vows, they must include certain elements in a Catholic marriage ceremony. First, the priest asks the couple several questions to establish that they are participating freely and know what they are getting into. Second, the bride and groom give their consent: they state their feelings for each other and make their vows. Third, they exchange rings as an outward symbol of their feelings for each other and for the marriage they are entering.

On our own wedding day, we used standard vows. We were lucky to have our friend and campus minister from college, Fr. Conrad Kratz, OPraem, celebrate our wedding Mass. As part of the Catholic Rite of Marriage, he asked us, "Have you come here feely and without reservation to give yourselves to each other in marriage?" We answered, "Yes." Then he questioned each of us: "Will you love and honor each other as man and wife for the rest of your lives?" We replied, "Yes." Then he asked us, "Will you accept children lovingly from God, and bring them up according to the law of Christ and his Church?" (This portion may be omitted in the case of older couples or in special circumstances.) Again, we said, "Yes."

We then joined right hands and promised each other, "I, Andrew, take you, Amy, to be my wife. I promise to be true to you in good times and in bad, in sickness and in health. I will love you and honor you all the days of my life." Then, "I, Amy, take you, Andrew, to be my husband. I promise to be true to you in good times and in bad, in sickness and in health. I will love you and honor you all the days of my life."

Fr. Conrad then said, "You have declared your consent before the Church. May the Lord in his goodness strengthen your consent and fill you both with his blessings. What God has joined, men must not divide."

He took and blessed the rings, and we placed them on each other's finger, saying, "Take this ring as a sign of my love and fidelity." We actually screwed this part up, and one of us ended up with the ring on the wrong hand, but Fr. Conrad assured us that it counted nonetheless. We then got to kiss each other for the first time as a married couple.

Looking again at these vows, we are struck by their simplicity, beauty, and profundity. Every couple who go through this rite say to each other, "I love and trust you so much that I'm giving myself to you freely." Within this context of freedom of choice, they express to each other something about what is inside them, what they feel: love and fidelity. They make a pledge of what they will do: love, honor, and be true. They say *when* they will do and feel these things: all the days of our life. Notice that they do not say, "From now on or for the rest of our life." They are more specific than that. Which days do they have to do these things? *All* the days: *every single day.*

Consider this statement for a minute. Think of the things you do every single day. The list is pretty small: you breathe. Sure, you eat and sleep on most days, but there are occasions when you are too sick to eat or too troubled to sleep. This is not an option insofar as your love, honor, and fidelity toward your spouse are concerned. You cannot say, "Sorry, honey, I just don't feel up to honoring you today," or, "I'm so preoccupied with this crisis at work that I don't have any energy left for fidelity. Check back next week."

You do not
take vacations from marriage.

You do not take vacations from marriage. You are to love, honor, and be true to your spouse "in good times and in bad, in sickness and in health." On your wedding day, you essentially choose freely, before God and the church, to promise your spouse that from this moment forth you will be a different person, one who not only breathes every day but also loves, honors, and is true to your spouse *every day.*

The Format of This Book

This book is intended to help you focus on these wedding vows and see how they provide the context within which all other marriage issues exist. Marriage vows, when lived daily, sustain a relationship through the challenges that life presents. Each chapter title is from the Catholic Rite of Marriage. Over the course of these chapters, we describe how we and other couples we know live these vows every day *and* how these vows, which for the nervous couple-to-be may seem daunting or even impossible beforehand (especially in *sickness* and *bad* times), actually become the glue that binds the marriage together (*especially* in sickness and bad times). We will also describe the effect on our own life together when we forget to live these vows daily as we should (hint: it is not good).

Marriage vows, when lived daily,
sustain a relationship
through the challenges
that life presents.

Chapter 1—"Have You Come Here Freely and Without Reservation to Give Yourselves to Each Other in Marriage?"—focuses on preparing for marriage and realizing that marriage is the gift of yourself, given freely and without reservation, to your spouse. It looks at reasons for marriage and considers its benefits as well.

Chapter 2—"I Promise to Be True to You"—examines what it means to be true to your spouse and how couples live their marital fidelity and trustworthiness every day.

Chapter 3—"In Good Times and in Bad, in Sickness and in Health"—discusses some of the things that young couples preparing for marriage do not like to think about: sources of trouble in marriage and how commitment to your spouse can sustain marriage through the good and the bad.

Saint Paul said, "Faith, hope, and love abide, these three; and the greatest of these is love" (1 Corinthians 13:13). Chapter 4—"I Will Love You and Honor You"—looks at how love develops and grows over the course of a marriage. This chapter also considers the role of honor and mutual respect in marriage.

Finally, chapter 5—"All the Days of My Life"—talks about growing and changing together and looks at how life's changes, such as childbirth, parenting, and aging, provide opportunities to live the wedding vows every day and expand them to include children.

We hope that by the time you finish this book, you will glimpse what married life is like, at least for some people, and that reading about our experiences and those of other married couples will develop in you a greater appreciation for Catholic marriage as it is being lived today. If you gain insight into how to deal effectively with or avoid problems that may arise in any marriage, we will have accomplished something worthwhile. For those of you who are getting ready to marry, we hope that reading this book will remind you to balance wedding plans with marriage plans, so that your happiness will last a lot longer than a day. As the wonderful, traditional Jewish wedding toast says, "May this day be the unhappiest day of your life!"

"Have You Come Here Freely and Without Reservation to Give Yourselves to Each Other in Marriage?"

Preparing for the Marriage You Will Live

At the opening of the Catholic Rite of Marriage, the priest asks the bride and groom to affirm that they are present because they want to be and that they really want to go through with the ceremony. Imagine if the question were asked differently: "Have you come here begrudgingly or because someone is forcing you, and do you have some nagging doubts about whether you are making the right decision?" Somewhat less romantic, to be sure, but this is essentially what is being asked. It is a vital question.

A few years back, a man we know confided in us his recollection of his one recurring thought leading up to and on his wedding day: "This is a mistake." He wrote off his concerns as the normal nervousness experienced by most (if not all) grooms and chided himself to "be a man." He did not talk to anyone about it at the time, because—well, he is a man, and today's culture tells men not to ask for help.

As the wedding day drew near, he found it harder and harder to bring up his doubts to anyone because so many people had invested time, effort, and money in the wedding. The bridesmaids had had their dresses tai-lored; the parents had made nonrefundable deposits on the wedding hall and disc jockey; the couple had purchased airline tickets for the honey-moon, and so on. Plus, he was afraid of how his fiancée might react; she would likely be hurt and even angry. Of course, he did not want to be the bad guy, so he pressed on, even though he needed a couple of drinks before the wedding to get through it.

Not surprisingly, this couple struggled. After about ten years of what (looking back on it) they both considered "living a lie," they went through a painful separation and an eventual divorce.

Another couple we know were in a similar predicament as their wedding day approached. The difference in this case is that the bride said something to the groom just three days before the wedding. To her relief, the groom replied that he had been experiencing similar doubts, and they decided to call off the wedding. Although they had to endure some embarrassment at having to announce the cancellation and had to deal with giving back wedding gifts and attempting to get refunds for many of the expenses, they both agreed that these were minor inconvenienc-es when compared to entering a marriage they felt they should not be in. By the way, both have since gone on to marry someone else and are very happy.

Why Get Married?

If our first couple had been honest with themselves and with each other about being there freely and giving themselves without reservation, they could have saved themselves many years of frustration. Marriage is too important and is supposed to last too long for people to get married for the wrong reasons, as the first couple did. There are lots of bad reasons to get married and really only one good one.

The bad reasons that we have heard of include:
- "All of our friends always expected us to get married."
- "Our parents want us to get married."
- "I feel too guilty or embarrassed to call it off at this point."
- "We're pregnant."
- "Two can live more cheaply than one."

- "I'm afraid of growing old alone."
- "All of my friends are getting married."
- "I always wanted to have a big wedding, like Princess Diana's."
- "I need to marry him to change him into a responsible person."
- "I don't want her to run off with someone else."
- "I want to have sex, and she won't without a ring."
- "I want someone to do my laundry and cook for me."
- "I want a child."
- "My fiancée has tremendous earning potential."

"Have you come here freely? Do you give yourself without reservation?"

If you look back at this list of reasons, you might notice that they all have something in common: each violates one or both of the two questions posed in the first part of the marriage vows. Have you come here freely? Do you give yourself without reservation? Several bad reasons at the top of the list involve marrying as a result of external pressure from friends, parents, peers, economics, or society (and, yes, even the church). These people marry under duress, not freely. Historically speaking, freedom in marriage is a relatively recent development, one that the church has embraced in its Rite of Marriage that is necessary for the sacrament of marriage to take place.

A document of Vatican Council II states that marriage "is rooted in the conjugal covenant of irrevocable personal consent" (*Pastoral Constitution on the Church in the Modern World,* no. 48). A priest we know, who has handled a number of annulment cases, tells us that the annulment of many marriages is based on the premise that the marriage was not entered with mature consent, that is, not freely. Both partners must freely choose marriage in order for it to be a holy act. The folks at the head of our list of bad reasons have not yet reached that point.

The reasons in the latter portion of the list sound like those of people who are taking, not giving. These people hope to profit somehow from their marriage, to take from their partner more than they plan to give.

If you are preparing for marriage, it is important to keep track of what is going through your head. Are you thinking of all the ways that you will benefit from the marriage or of what you plan to give to it? Of course, you go into marriage expecting to be happy (this is a normal experience before—and during—a marriage), but you ought to reflect seriously on whether this happiness is based more on what you expect to gain than on what you expect to share. A marriage that one or both partners enter for purely selfish reasons fails to meet the church's definition of marriage. (Saint Paul has some interesting things to say about this topic in chapter 7 of the First Letter to the Corinthians.)

Marriage is a vocation.

Marriage is a vocation, like entering the priesthood, becoming a sister or a brother, or living a single life. If a man were to enter the priesthood primarily because of the financial benefits of the job, you would say that he will not make a good priest, because he is going into it for the wrong reasons (and you might add that he needs a new career counselor). The same is true for marriage.

We promise to try, for most of this book, to avoid telling you what to do, but in this case we are making an exception. Do not get married out of guilt; doing so generally creates more problems than it solves. Do not get married to please someone else; you are likely to end up resenting the person you are trying to please. Do not get married for financial reasons; the short-term financial benefits will be offset by the costly divorce you are likely to go through later. Besides, you deserve love in your marriage, not just money. Do not get married to have a baby; kids have a tough enough time without bearing the burden of having to be the glue that holds a marriage together.

Although marriage is an extremely complicated lifestyle that requires two people to enter one life and to adjust, grow, and mature together, the reason for getting into it is really quite simple. In our years of counseling couples in marriage preparation, in our conversations with family and friends, in our own experience, and in everything we have read about marriage, we have really heard only one good reason to get married. Please do not get married for any reason other than this one: *"We love each other, and we want to spend the rest of our life together."*

"Well, of course," you say. "That is why everyone gets married, isn't it?" Unfortunately, no. In addition to the weak reasons for marriage already mentioned, lots of folks get married without thinking about what a lifetime commitment really is. Many people, especially young people, mistake infatuation or sexual attraction for love. (We will look at love more closely in chapter 4.)

How can you know whether what you are feeling is genuine love or simply attraction? This is a tough question, and the answer will vary from person to person, from couple to couple. We will say this much: if you are a young person considering marriage, realize that there is little chance that your spouse will grow *more* physically attractive as you get older and a good chance that he or she will grow *less* so. This is just how humans work: hair grays, muscles soften, skin wrinkles, and gravity prevails over all. So as you and your spouse mature, you had better have something more powerful than physical attractiveness or infatuation to sustain your marriage.

Do not get us wrong; people who are in love will continue to be physically attracted to each other as they grow older and, if physically healthy, will usually maintain a happy sexual relationship. We know elderly married couples who are deeply in love and still find each other very attractive. But people whose relationship is based *primarily* on physical attraction will grow bored, probably even before any signs of aging are noticeable.

As far as compatibility goes over the long haul, if you often find yourself bickering about little things—like what movies to see, what share of time to spend with each other and with friends, and what radio station to play in the car—imagine what life will be like when you have mortgage payments, in-laws, and child rearing to deal with.

A common mistake that couples make going into a marriage is to think that their typical way of interacting will change after they are married. This is rarely the case. Couples who are rude to each other before marriage are just as likely to continue being rude to each other afterward. Those who are kind and respectful to each other beforehand will probably experience more of the same once they are married.

What is the infatuation-to-love ratio in your relationship?

Here is a little test to help you determine the infatuation-to-love ratio in your relationship. Look at your partner. Now look at your partner's parents. Will you still want to be with your partner when she or he looks like that? Loving the whole person—physical, emotional, rational—is essential if that person is the one with whom you plan to spend the rest of your life. An ironic aspect of human behavior is that physical attraction usually draws the person to the partner in the first place, but physical attraction in itself is almost never enough to sustain a long-term relationship. If you and your spouse are going to spend the rest of your life together (that is how marriage is supposed to work), it is important that you love your partner.

Getting Ready for Marriage

To increase the likelihood that the marriage will indeed last a lifetime, the Catholic church requires (except in special circumstances) that couples planning a wedding in the church participate in one of several pre-Cana programs. The primary purposes of pre-Cana marriage preparation are to determine that the bride- and groom-to-be are indeed getting married for the right reasons, that they are doing so freely, that they have similar expectations for the marriage, and that they will go to the altar without any reservations. A good pre-Cana counselor or counseling couple will listen without judging and will encourage the engaged couple to determine honestly whether getting married is the correct thing for them to do at the moment.

Pre-Cana marriage preparation should be a period of discernment.

A pre-Cana program should not recruit people into marriage, discourage expressions of doubt, or take a "full steam ahead" attitude toward the wedding. On the contrary, the program should be a period of discernment, a time for the couple to reflect on their values, needs, and expectations. In a pre-Cana counseling session, the engaged couple should do most of the talking, and they should converse primarily with each other. Most of the couples we have counseled have tended to try to talk to us during the sessions. When they do, we gently remind them that *we* are not marrying them, so we are not the ones to whom they should direct their comments. If you ever find yourself in a pre-Cana situation where you feel that you are not being heard by your partner or that the counselor couple want to spend the time talking about themselves and their own marriage, change your counselor or try a different program. Parishes usually offer more than one option.

After completing a Catholic marriage preparation program, you should feel and know one of two alternatives: "I'm ready to give myself to my partner freely and without reservation" or "I'm not ready for marriage right now." Believe it or not, both are successful pre-Cana outcomes. Our own pre-Cana experience resulted in the affirmation of our plans to marry.

*"I'm ready to give myself
to my partner
freely and without reservation."*

We know a man whose pre-Cana sessions with his fiancée had a different result: he is now a Catholic priest. This couple's discernment led them to conclude that they were being called in very different directions, a fact they are now glad to have discovered before getting married.

The only way you can fail at marriage preparation is to go into a marriage for which you are not ready. We do not mean to imply that if you are ready for marriage, you will not be nervous. Indeed, if you are not a little nervous, you may not be experiencing the enormity of what you are doing. If you are not sure whether your nervousness is "normal" or reflects serious doubts, it is a good idea to talk about it. Remember our friend from the beginning of the chapter? Avoid making the mistake he and his fiancée made. Talk with your friends, your parents, your priest, your pre-Cana counselors, and most important of all, your partner. (If you are going to get married, you are going to talk about a lot of sensitive issues in your life together; you may as well get used to it.)

For us and for other couples we know, the ability to talk with each other about our feelings as we prepared for marriage was one indication that we were actually ready to take this step and to give ourselves to each other.

The Greatest Gift

Some couples follow a tradition where the bride and groom buy each other a wedding gift. Although this is a nice gesture, it is also, in our opinion, redundant. What gift could be greater than to dedicate yourself to your partner for the rest of your life? When you stand before the altar in front of your friends, your family, your church, and your God, stating that you are there freely and give yourself to your partner without reservation, you publicly declare that your trust in this person is absolute. (We will look more at trustworthiness in the next chapter.)

After you and your partner offer yourself to each other, you declare in the next line of your vows that you accept this precious gift, just as we did: "I, Amy, take you, Andrew, to be my husband." The gift of yourself, given freely, sets the stage for the vows you are about to make to your partner, the promises you are about to declare, and the life together you are about to begin.

After the wedding it is important to recognize that you continue to give the gift of yourself freely to your spouse every day. Every activity you do for your spouse is a gift of time and effort, your time and effort donated to your partner. From little things to big things and everything in between—tickling your spouse's back while you read in bed, taking a shirt to the dry cleaner, listening carefully to a problem experienced at work, filling the car with gas because you know your spouse needs it the next day, shopping for groceries, sharing your paycheck, giving a hug after a tough day, making love, serving breakfast in bed, going out for a night on the town, telling a well-timed joke to make your spouse laugh, cleaning the kitchen, squeezing a hand quickly under the table at a dinner party, kissing as the first thing in the morning or the last thing at night, giving a sign of peace during Mass, making a phone call in the middle of the day to say hi, sneaking a love note someplace where your spouse will find it later, doing the laundry, admitting "I'm sorry" after a fight, saying "I love you" anytime—these are all gifts that are appreciated as such.

These actions and countless others, including the gift of children, are the constant donations of self that constitute a marriage. The happiest marriages are those where both partners freely bestow and appreciatively accept these gifts. Even in happy marriages, the times when tension does arise are often those when the couple do not appreciate gifts, bestow them begrudgingly, or both.

Showing Gratitude

We describe our own marriage as being a very happy one. This does not mean that our life is a constant stream of uninterrupted bliss. We have disagreements, arguments, and periods of resentment and anger like everyone else (at least we are pretty sure everyone else has these, too).

Over the years, we have discovered at least two things about these periodic bouts with dysfunction. First, they almost always occur when one of us has been unappreciative of the gifts the other has given: criticizing the dinner rather than being thankful for the effort involved in making it, complaining about the bills rather than being grateful for the services they represent, complaining about time spent at work rather than being thankful for the effort to provide for the family, not noticing the energy one spouse has put into a project that benefits both—that sort of thing. The underappreciated one is usually hurt by the complaints and may react with anger or sadness. Sometimes the situation escalates into harsh words, more hurt feelings, and other not-so-fun aspects of the relationship.

Second, these difficulties are usually resolved easily. Typically, all it takes is for the offending person to recognize the insensitivity that was shown and then to apologize. Of course, considerable prompting is sometimes required before the offending person achieves this recognition, and stubbornness at times delays the offer of an apology. But so far in our marriage, the recognition and the resulting apology have always come, and with them a renewed appreciation of how much we do for each other every day.

Our purpose in this chapter is to emphasize the importance of freely entering a marriage and of giving yourself to your partner throughout your marriage. It is not accidental that these free decisions are the first portion of the marriage vows. They are the preconditions for the promises stated in the rest of the marriage vows.

Without these preconditions—freedom of choice and gift of self— the other portions of the vows make no sense. "I have serious doubts about this, but I will love you forever," doesn't quite work. One person says, "I freely give myself to you." What greater act of love is there? The other responds, "I take you, and I promise to be true to you." What response could be more appropriate? In the next chapter, we will look at what it means to be true to each other.

Chapter 2

"I Promise to Be True to You"

Living a Life of Faithfulness and Fidelity

In the film *True Lies,* the character played by Jamie Lee Curtis thinks that her husband, acted by Arnold Schwarzenegger, is just an average guy going off each day to work for a computer firm. As it turns out, he is an international spy who almost daily risks his life in the name of national intelligence. Although this story is an extreme example, we use it here to illustrate the importance of the first promise of the wedding vows: to be true. Was Arnold being true to Jamie Lee? We think not. He was not having an affair with someone else, which is what usually comes to mind when people talk about infidelity, but he was lying to her every time he left for work.

This concept of being true is a complex one; let's look at it a bit before discussing how it applies to marriage. Merriam-Webster notes that the word *true* comes from the Old English word *treowe,* which means *faithful.* In the Rite of Marriage, the couple exchange rings as a sign of their love and fidelity. Fidelity comes from the Latin word *fidelis,* which (you might remember from the Christmas carol) also means *faithful.* Truth and fidelity have a common root, a common idea, as their origin: faithfulness.

What does it mean to be faithful?

What does it mean to be faithful, and how can you live faithfulness every day? Basically, when you are being faithful, you are being the person your spouse believes you to be. In the film we described earlier, the husband is not being faithful to his wife. He is someone she does not really know. Of course, she accidentally finds out about his "real" life. The two of them have a series of thrilling adventures involving spectacular, costly special effects and breathtaking stunts, until they gross millions at the box office, which in Hollywood is what it means to live happily ever after.

High Fidelity

Hollywood contributes significantly to society's understanding of fidelity. People, bombarded with movie and television images of married men and women having sexual relations with someone other than their spouse, are lulled into feeling that this is all there is to marital fidelity or infidelity (and that this form of infidelity is pretty much the norm in marriages). They conclude that if they do not have sex with someone else, they are being faithful, or true, to their partner.

Although having a sexual relationship with someone other than your spouse certainly is a violation of marital trust, sexual activity is only a part of what constitutes genuine fidelity. Faithfulness is a much bigger issue than simply where and with whom a person sleeps. When you say to your spouse at the altar, "I promise to be true to you," you are in essence saying, "I promise to be honest with you and to be the person I seem to be." Seems obvious, doesn't it? But things don't always turn out that way.

We know a certain couple who have been married for many years. Several years ago, Andy was with the husband and had just finished playing a round of golf. In the clubhouse afterward, our friend sat on a bar stool and phoned his wife. He told her that they had gotten a late start and the course was crowded, so they had just completed the first nine holes and still had nine to go. (Remember that in reality they had already finished the entire eighteen holes.) As he said this, he smiled and winked at the bartender and a few other men seated nearby. It would be another two to three hours before they finished, he told her; then he would come right home. He seated himself in a card game. When one of the players asked why he did not simply tell his wife he was playing cards, the husband responded, "She doesn't like my gambling. Besides, if she knew I was here, she might try to call."

If you were to ask this man whether he was being unfaithful to his wife, he would place his hand on a Bible and swear that he was not. He was not sleeping with these men; he was playing cards with them. Where was the harm in that? Well, the harm lies not necessarily in the act of playing cards (although some people would argue that gambling *is* harmful or even sinful) but in the act of willfully deceiving his wife. He lied to her, and he did it in a room full of people, possibly placing them in an awkward position if they were to meet his wife later. His wink and his smile told us that he knew full well what he was doing, yet he went right on doing it. We don't know if she ever found out about this particular deception, but we are sure that if she did, she was hurt, angry, and embarrassed.

Are we suggesting that married people have to give up the things they like to do if their spouse does not like their doing it? No, not necessarily. We are suggesting that married couples should learn to be honest with each other about themselves, their likes and dislikes, their hobbies and pastimes, their fears and aspirations. Sharing these aspects brings a couple closer together.

We think this husband should have been more honest with his wife about how he was spending his time. They should have talked about it before he went to the golf course so that the deceptive phone call would not have been necessary. It is possible that if he had been honest with his wife, this man may have been surprised at her acceptance of his spending time with his friends, and she may have been interested in spending more time with her friends. Maybe not.

Because this couple had been married a long time, it is likely that this incident was not isolated but one in a long series. Because behavior patterns, once established, tend to perpetuate themselves in a marriage, the early formation of truthful habits of interaction is important to a successful long-term relationship.

Of course, if a person has a behavior that is genuinely destructive to the marriage—excessive drinking, irresponsible gambling, compulsive shopping, drug abuse, violence, and so on—simply being honest about it is not enough to prevent damaging the marriage. Elimination of the problem behavior (probably with outside professional help) would be necessary. As we suggested in the previous chapter, young people getting ready for marriage should realize that problem behaviors in their partner will almost certainly *not* just go away after they are married.

What About Avoidance?

Some of you may suggest that the card-playing golfer should not have called his wife at all. He could have avoided lying to her simply by not speaking to her. After all, what he does with his time is none of her business. Being truthful is more than what you say; not saying anything is often clearly an act of deceit. Remember, he told us that he knew his wife did not want him to gamble. His doing so was an act of infidelity toward her, whether or not he lied to her about it.

Consider this example: if a married woman is having an affair, telling her husband that she is out shopping at the time is also an unfaithful act, although most people would agree that it is the less significant of the two. It is important to recognize in marriage that acts of omission—that is, not doing or saying something you should—as well as acts of commission—doing or saying something you know you should not—are both potential sources of marital infidelity.

What About Privacy?

Isn't a spouse entitled to some privacy? Good point. Do married couples give up their right to privacy when they wed? We think that it is important for couples to distinguish between privacy and secrecy. For example, when we were first married, we did not agree on the issue of mail. One of us thought that mail was for the person to whom it was addressed. The other did not believe there was anything wrong with opening each other's mail, there being no secrets between us, after all. To settle matters, we had to have a lengthy discussion that involved our assurances to each other about trust and respect.

We resolved the problem by basically agreeing that mail is private and for the person to whom it is addressed and that we would no more read each other's mail than we would listen in on each other's phone conversations (a habit practiced by some couples we know). By agreeing to this solution, we affirmed to each other our mutual trust, again living our vows. Ironically, we now receive the bulk of our mail addressed to both of us; it generally consists of bills and solicitations by credit card companies and sits on the kitchen counter for days at a time, unopened by either one of us.

What About White Lies?

Wait a minute. What about hurt feelings? Maybe it was an act of kindness for the golfer-turned-card-player to lie to his wife about what he was doing. Because he did not want to hurt her, he did not tell her the truth. Our reply is that if telling the truth about what you are doing will hurt your spouse, you probably should not be doing it.

This example brings up something else that a lot of people in relationships have to come to terms with: white lies, those little deviations from the truth that people use to avoid conflicts or uncomfortable situations. A neighbor asks your opinion of the drapes he has just hung, drapes you wouldn't use to clean the grease off a car engine, for fear of ruining the grease. "How well they go with this carpet," you manage to respond, realizing that the carpet is even more hideous than the drapes.

You have not told your neighbor your true feelings, but that is not what is called for in this relationship. White lies are based on the social assumption that politeness is sometimes more important than the absolute truth. Courtesy is not a bad thing, of course, but it can be somewhat superficial. We hope that a marital relationship or one in preparation for marriage goes beyond superficiality or mere good manners. The depth of feeling in a marriage should render white lies unnecessary.

Does this mean that you should go through life being brutally honest with your spouse? "Gee, honey, that dress really makes you look fat." "Oh, I wouldn't apply for that job, dear; I just don't think you've got the brains for it." "Boy, you sure are starting to look old!" What do you think? We do not believe that honesty, truthfulness, and fidelity have to be tactless and insensitive, but neither can we sacrifice honesty, truthfulness, and fidelity for the sake of tact or sensitivity.

Consider this scenario: A husband has purchased a bright pink scarf as a birthday gift for his wife. She hates it and would sooner burn it than wear it. The honest but insensitive wife opens the gift and responds, "I hate it and would sooner burn it than wear it," thereby hurting her husband's feelings and turning what should have been a positive exchange for both of them into a negative one for him.

The sensitive but dishonest wife says, "I love it," and places it in a drawer, where it collects dust, and condemns herself to an eventual drawerful of dusty scarves, all gifts from her husband that she does not want and will never wear.

The sensitive and honest wife tries to balance her husband's feelings and her own. She might say something like this, "Honey, I am so grateful that you thought of me and spent time getting me this gift; you are so thoughtful. I only wish it were a color that I am more comfortable wearing. How about if we go out together tomorrow, and you can help me exchange it for something that matches more of the clothes I have?"

The husband might be a little put out by this response, but at least he knows that she appreciates the thought and effort he put into the gift. The two of them can go exchange the gift, and he can learn more about his wife's tastes—which will help him the next time he buys something for her.

Live life truthfully
and draw together
in faithfulness.

In the short term, the second option would certainly be easier for the sensitive wife to do, but in the long run, we think option three is better. It allows couples to live their life truthfully and draw together in faithfulness.

We know a man who traveled from his home in Wisconsin to Florida to help his brother paint his house. To thank him after the job was finished, the brother and his wife took the man out to dinner. (The Wisconsin man's wife had not made the trip.)

Shortly after dinner began, the waiter presented the man with a note written in an unfamiliar but identifiably a woman's hand, which read, "I think you are a very handsome man and would like to buy you a drink." The man looked at the note and returned it to the waiter, indicating that he would not accept. The waiter mentioned that it was a woman in the bar area of the restaurant and gestured in that direction. The man declined, refusing even to look toward her. "Tell her thank you, but I am not interested," he instructed the waiter.

The waiter departed but returned a few minutes later, indicating that the woman insisted she would like to meet him just for a moment. Again the man declined and sent the waiter to tell her that he would not be joining her at the bar. Finally, the woman persisted and walked up to the table. It turned out that it was the man's own wife, who had flown down from Wisconsin to surprise her husband, with help from the brother and his wife, who had written the note. She had hoped that her husband would look up to identify the woman buying him a drink and then see her.

Her plans to surprise him did not go as she had intended, but she was actually very pleased with the way it turned out. This man still carries the "mystery" note in his wallet. His act of faithfulness to his wife affirmed the strength of their marriage.

Fate, Choice, or Accident?

Hollywood movies, television, and popular fiction often depict marital infidelity as some sort of an accident or fated event. Two people find themselves together, and there is instant chemistry that they cannot resist. We do not know anyone who has experienced marital infidelity that happens like that. The people we know who have encountered marital infidelity firsthand all acknowledge that their infidelity is an act of will, almost always premeditated—as it was in the case of our golfing card-player.

One woman we know, whose husband had an affair that led to the end of their marriage, relates that the physical relationship her husband had with another woman was not the most upsetting part of this painful event in her life. Instead it was his ongoing and willful deception that hurt her the most. She thought she was married to a certain man, but it turned out he was someone quite different than the man she assumed she knew. This man's faithlessness had begun long before his physical relationship with the other woman. It started when he began deceiving his wife to spend time with that woman.

Being true
is being consistent.

Being true is being consistent. People who are in the habit of faithfulness to their spouse, like the man from Wisconsin, find it easy to be faithful because they do not often place themselves in situations where their fidelity is put to the test. When they occasionally find themselves in such circumstances, their faithfulness is strong enough to see them through without succumbing. Being false often involves putting yourself in a situation that is likely to lead to infidelity and then pretending that it "just happened."

A prominent politician once made the comment, "I never lie, because I'm not smart enough." What he meant is that deception complicates your life. If you lie, you have to keep track of your lies. There is almost never such a thing as a single act of deception. Lies need to be supported by other lies, which get woven into a tangled web. You ensnare yourself in them, and they end up controlling you.

Mental health experts advise people to simplify their lives. The fact is plain: "The truth will set you free." Living simply allows you to be truthful. Let us express this thought another way: in a marriage the important thing is not to avoid lying to your spouse but to avoid doing things that compel you to lie.

There is an analogy in today's society. Every once in a while, for instance, the question of overcrowded prisons re-enters the realm of political conversation. One group recommends building more prisons to relieve overcrowding and thereby be more humane to the prisoners. Another group counters by arguing that prisoners deserve to be overcrowded, that they bring it on themselves by breaking the law. Both groups fail to recognize that crime prevention in the first place would render prisons unnecessary.

So it is in a marriage: the argument should not be about telling your spouse that you have committed a marital transgression but about avoiding the offense in the first place. When you pledge, "I promise to be true to you," you are referring to much more than what you are saying; otherwise, the vow would be something like "I swear to tell the truth, the whole truth, and nothing but the truth, so help me God." You promise not only to *tell* what is true but to *be* true.

Being Faith-Filled

Of course, another meaning for the term faithfulness refers to the way you live out your belief in God. This aspect, too, is part of the marriage vows. In chapter 5 we will discuss the element of the vows that involves accepting children and raising them in faith, but you will live your faith in your relationship before you have any children.

Like other marital habits you develop, your religious practices will guide you in decision making and help you define yourself as a good and honorable person. Going to church, praying together, celebrating the sacraments—these are all part of living as the person you are, that is, being true to your spouse, your faith, and yourself.

Social psychologist Daryl Bem has coined the useful term "self-perception theory" to highlight a process over time whereby people come to understand who they are. They do this, so the theory goes, by recalling and cognitively organizing their past behaviors. If you practice your faith and your faithfulness regularly, you will come to perceive yourself and believe in yourself as trustworthy and honest. If you find yourself in a situation where you are not sure how to act or where others are acting as you think they should not, you examine your previous actions and use them to guide your current ones.

A woman who lies regularly to her spouse develops this habit, and it will guide her to act the same way in new situations. On the other hand, a woman who is regularly truthful with her husband will perceive herself as an honest person and act accordingly.

The man from Wisconsin who helped his brother in Florida had never been in a situation of being approached by a woman other than his wife (and it turns out he still hasn't). So how did he know what to do? As he tells it, he examined his conscience and thought about his wife. He decided it would be inappropriate to accept an offer of a drink or an invitation to join another woman. In his mind, doing so would have been an act of deception and a violation of his marital vows. It would have made it difficult to be completely honest with his wife the next time they were together, so he avoided placing himself in this situation. It turned out that his wife's trust in him was well placed.

Trust is
an extraordinary experience.

Trust is an extraordinary experience. Like love, it is a gift from God, and we would argue that it is every bit as important in a successful and happy marriage as love is. We know couples whose relationship ended not because they stopped loving each other but because they stopped trusting each other. Marriage without trust promotes jealousy and suspicion, which poison a relationship.

If you tell a friend something personal about yourself and then find out that he has shared it with someone else, your relationship will be damaged. At the very least, it will be a long, long time before you trust him again with something important to you. So it is in marriage. If you violate your spouse's trust in you, it will take a lot of time and effort to restore that trust. Some argue that trust is like fine china—easily damaged and, once broken, never fully restorable to its original condition.

Another aspect of trust is that if you are untrue to your spouse and your spouse does *not* find out, you have still done damage to your relationship. "What you don't know won't hurt you" does not apply in a marriage. The only effective way to re-establish trust in a relationship is through forgiveness, but you can never have forgiveness if one person is unaware that forgiveness is needed.

In this chapter we have tried to describe both the many ways that married couples live the vow, "I promise to be true to you," and some of the unfortunate consequences when marital partners do not live it. We have talked about the habits of marriage and how couples early in their marriage often establish marital habits that will last a lifetime.

These are especially important considerations for those of you contemplating marriage. Do you trust your partner? Are you ready to accept the enormous responsibility of the trust your partner is placing in you? If so, you are probably ready to consider marriage. If not, you must do more searching about these matters in preparation for your marriage.

The only marriage we can think of that would be more difficult than a loveless one would be a trustless one. On the other hand, a marriage based on absolute trust is a joyful experience, a genuine friendship, and a lifelong comfort.

"In Good Times and in Bad, in Sickness and in Health"

Love and Faith in Times of Trouble

In the midst of the joy and excitement of their wedding day, some couples operate under one of two possible misconceptions as they confront the future. Some have the nagging feeling that life is all downhill from here—the freedom is gone; marital spats, conflict, and struggles lie ahead; surely no day in the future could be as exuberantly fun and exciting as this one.

What is especially disheartening, we think, is that popular culture often ascribes this bleak view to the husband and supports the common metaphors that describe husbands as strapping on a "ball and chain" or being "henpecked." At a wedding ceremony one of us attended, someone used masking tape on the soles of the groom's shoes to spell out the word *help* for all the congregation to see as he knelt at the altar.

We experienced this attitude on the occasion of our own wedding, when we went to the airport to pick up one of the attendants. The groomsman stepped off the plane and announced to the nervous groom, "Just think, only forty-eight hours and it's nag, nag, nag till the day you die."

Popular television shows like *Married with Children* depict couples dissatisfied with each other, sarcastic, and critical. Although we recognize that all these attitudes are aimed at getting a laugh, they do represent a belief that married life is really not much fun, especially for the husband.

Under the second misconception, on the other hand, some couples blissfully gaze into the future and see only a scene of domestic utopia. When we succumbed to this misconception, sometimes we would see ourselves in a perfect suburban home with a white picket fence, a cozy fireplace, several happy, loving children, and a family dog. At other times we fantasized about living an exciting life abroad in a foreign city with interesting, important careers, several happy, loving children, and a family dog. No matter the setting, we fervently believed that we and our imagined offspring would always be happy (and for reasons we cannot quite remember, a dog always figured into it). Life would always turn out as we planned, and it was only going to get better from this day forward.

On the occasions when popular culture depicts matrimony as a good thing, the story usually leaves marital bliss to the imagination, ends with the wedding scene, and implies (or states outright) a "happy ever after" sentiment.

Life Has Its Ups and Downs

The reality for us—and, we think, the reality for most couples—is that the future (thus far) turns out to be a combination of good and bad times. Indeed at times we feel nagged, sense a loss of independence, or even feel like calling for help, like the unsuspecting groom with the masking tape on his soles. Every married couple we know experiences this reaction at some point. Sometimes the two just cannot see eye to eye on anything. At other times the world, the fates, or some force seems dead set on bringing them hardship. Almost all marriages have rocky spells.

Conversely, if yours turns out to be one of the rare weddings that goes off without a single hitch, you can rejoice in the fact that nearly all couples will have many more "perfect" and once-in-a-lifetime days ahead. There will be events that rival your wedding day in excitement and bursting-with-pride joy, such as the first home, job hirings and promotions, and the birth of children.

The future turns out to be a combination of good and bad times.

Many couples report that the happiest day of their life is not the day they get married but the day when a child enters their life, whether through birth or adoption. Your children and their accomplishments will, in turn, be the source of many happy days for you: first tooth, first step, first word, First Communion, graduation, wedding, and so on.

Other days may not be momentous enough to be red-letter days on the calendar but contribute to the good times nonetheless: walking through the leaves on a beautiful fall afternoon, enjoying a relaxing family vacation, engaging in sporting activities together, reading stories as a family, finishing a home-remodeling project, participating in family holiday customs, and having your children surprise you when they complete a task or do something so genuinely thoughtful and mature that it makes you want to cry. Frankly, at times a couple will be so obviously happy being together and in love that it will sicken those around them just to look at them!

The good news for us is that because we have stayed faithful to our commitment to each other, the good times have considerably outweighed the bad ones. If we charted our marriage on a graph, we think it would look a lot like the stock market over recent decades. Although periodically there have been significant dips and even an occasional crash, the overall trend is upward. Like the stock market over the long haul, our marriage investment has yielded significant returns and is in a much better position now than five, ten, or more years ago. We believe married life can continue that pattern. Life is not perfect, and we are not always happy, but it does keep getting better and better.

Precisely because most couples do experience highs and lows in their marriage, the vows ask them to declare their commitment to each other for both the good and the bad times. The act of commitment in itself has helped sustain us in our bad times.

Actions Speak Louder than Words

Simply saying that you will remain true through the bad times is not enough, however. The words are important, but actions, as the old saying goes, speak louder than words. Fortunately, our pre-Cana marriage preparation provided a great deal of information about how to resolve conflict in our marriage. We learned a lot about "fighting fair," and we have tried to abide by certain rules when we are mad at each other. One rule is that we do not say or do things that cannot, in essence, be taken back. Although Jesus taught—and we believe—that *anything* can be forgiven, we have tried hard never to wound too deeply.

The trust on which a marriage is based leaves couples vulnerable to hurtful actions by either partner.

The trust on which a marriage is based leaves couples vulnerable to hurtful actions by either partner. It is an act of love to avoid taking advantage of that vulnerability when one partner is angry. For instance, no matter how angry, upset, frustrated, or hurt we are, we do not resort to attacking each other's weaknesses or areas we know the other is sensitive about. Neither of us has ever said "I hate you" to the other, although we're sure both of us have thought it at one time or another. We do not use four-letter words to get our message across. We have never resorted to physical violence—ever.

It is tragic that domestic violence is all too common today. Most couples who are in an abusive relationship find themselves there after having moved gradually toward it—beginning with cutting, hurtful words, then threats, then physical violence. Verbal and physical violence are not only wrong; they are illegal. If you find yourself involved as either a victim or a perpetrator, you should seek professional help immediately.

Instead of hitting below the belt, so to speak, we avoid accusations and try to focus on communicating our feelings to each other in the hope that our partner will remember how strong our love is and will care enough to do something about our hurt feelings. "Doing something" might mean an agreement to change behavior: "Okay, from now on, I'll try to remember to call you if I'm going to be late." We often need gentle reminders so that we can establish the desired behavior permanently.

In the early years of our marriage, this practice became something of a joke between us. Announcing the introductory phrase, "Just for future reference," was a gentle way for us to say to each other, "You are doing something that bugs me. Do you think you could please stop it?" Dealing with hurt feelings also means simply apologizing: "I'm sorry. I wasn't thinking of how worried you might be when I wasn't home on time."

Focus on your love for each other.

Perhaps you feel that you shouldn't have to call when you are late. You are your own person, after all, and you can take care of yourself. You don't like being told what to do. What then? We think it is crucial to examine priorities when desired behaviors continue to conflict. If loving your spouse and caring about his or her feelings is the most important thing to you, what you should do becomes obvious. Focus on your love for each other. Try to be unselfish. Try to be Christlike. Your conflicts will work out, we hope, if you bear these virtues in mind. In the example above, we think that easing our partner's worries with a quick phone call when either of us is late is more important—that is, a higher priority— than nursing the somewhat immature feeling that we do not want to be told what to do.

Some people think, as we did early in our marriage, that you can guarantee a fair fight by using rules like the "I statement" rule: when you are angry, begin your statement with "I" rather than "you." In principle this is a fine idea. For example, "I am feeling hurt and angry because I had dinner ready an hour ago and didn't know where you were" is better than "You are so inconsiderate when you don't call and are late; now dinner is ruined!" The first statement is an expression of your own feelings; the second, a blaming accusation and attack.

These rules alone obviously do not guarantee that the statement will not be hurtful or vindictive. "I feel that you are an insensitive jerk." "Oh, yeah? Well, I feel that you are a nagging cow." See? Preventing a couple from hurting each other takes more than mere rules. It demands the love of both people, combined with a good deal of maturity and self-control.

Many couples find themselves unprepared for another instance of good and bad times that can occur: the feelings that surface when things seem to be "better" for one spouse than for the other. In our experience this situation happens most often in the area of careers and is due to a variety of factors. Many couples decide together, as we did, that one person's career will become less of a priority when children enter the picture. Often it is the woman who quits working outside the home altogether, or one spouse may reduce her or his workload and professional responsibilities. In essence this person puts a career on hold until the children are in school or even older.

Bearing a greater responsibility for raising children and caring for the home is often a more difficult task than many careers (and certainly a more important task than most occupations). It tends to receive little recognition and external rewards and generally does not include salary and benefits for the worker—important signs of validation in today's society.

As the years go by, the spouse who did not put a career on hold receives annual salary and benefit increases, greater responsibilities at work, promotions, and even awards and other accolades. For the other person, happiness and pride for the spouse are tempered by feelings of discouragement, envy, or resentment (perhaps accompanied by guilt for having these feelings). Why should one spouse get all the credit when both work equally hard for the family's happiness? Communication, sensitivity, a supportive attitude, and frequent verbal encouragement are key factors on such occasions.

In our family we consider that Andy's proportionally larger paycheck and Amy's correspondingly smaller one represent the combined effort of both of us to support our family. Two paychecks signify the family income that we work together to earn. We make an effort to thank each other every day for what each has done to support the family, whether by making dinner, working hard at the office, or taking the children to the dentist. We share our successes and give credit to the one who earns recognition. We do not hesitate to make it known that each of us is "the wind beneath the wings" for the other. Finally, we remind ourselves that the choices we have made together reflect our values and priorities and that we wouldn't do it any other way if we were to do it over again.

Under Pressure

Because of our thorough pre-Cana marriage preparation, we thought we had considered how to handle the bad times. We had talked about how to resolve conflicts and how to "fight fair" (using "I statements," among other means). We knew that marital spats are inevitable and believed we were ready to handle these internal problems. When we agreed to be true in good times and in bad, in sickness and in health, we thought we knew what that promise entailed. We even had some experience with these situations going into our marriage.

Couples often face bad times that are the result of external factors beyond their control.

Couples often face bad times that are the result of external factors beyond their control. Through no fault of either marriage partner, some couples face trouble brought about by infertility, illness, the loss of a child or other loved one, difficult economic times, unlucky circumstances, the trials of their adolescent children, and so on. Although couples have some control over the "good times and bad" by the way they choose to act toward each other, we think that the "in sickness and in health" portion of the vows speaks to the difficulties in marriage that are caused by external factors over which couples have no control.

What is a couple to do when they have little or no control over a troublesome situation? The best remedy—the only remedy, we believe—for these times of "sickness" is prayer. As any caring parents of an adolescent can tell you, prayer becomes a significant part of their life (if it isn't already) when their children reach the teen years and become more and more independent. Parents can say whole rosaries waiting for a teenager to return safely home by curfew.

Couples who face a profound struggle with grief or loss often say that their faith and prayer are the only things that sustain them. We know a couple whose teenage daughter ran away from home. Their love for each other, along with the help of their friends, their pastor, and a good deal of prayer, supported them through this difficult period. Happily, they have resolved their differences with their daughter and are now closer than ever to her. The sickness in this family has healed, for the most part.

Another kind of "bad" or "sick" time is economic hardship. Most couples experience at some point in their marriage a period of what they consider to be economic adversity. In some cases it's just a matter of expectations or overextending themselves: "With our vacation bills coming in, I don't know how we're going to make the payment on the second car." In other instances a spouse loses a job or suffers an injury that prevents work, and the couple teeter on the brink of (or even slip into) poverty.

Some friends of ours tell of a time in their marriage when they were both out of work. With a couple of children to raise, they decided that they needed to go on welfare. They also relate that their love for each other provided the emotional support they needed to get through this difficult period in their life. When one of them was starting to get down about their circumstances, the other was able to provide just enough energy to pick the spouse up, and vice versa. Their commitment to each other and their faith in themselves and in God sustained them through to better times.

Bouts of emotional illness or relational sickness are common in marriages and families, but so are physical maladies. Minor illnesses like chicken pox, flu, or even the common cold place stress on family relationships, require an adjustment of routine, cause an inequitable distribution of workload, and create other inconveniences. Major illnesses like heart disease, cancer, or Alzheimer's disease can have devastating effects on relationships, drive couples apart, and propel them away from their faith.

In a powerful and moving scene in the film *Lorenzo's Oil*, the parents of a terminally ill child fight bitterly over the circumstances of his illness until one spouse accuses the other of causing the boy's disease. The tragic aspect for viewers is that they want this couple to remain strong for each other and for their sick son. In times of grave illness, families need their love for each other and their faith to be the strongest.

When times are at their worst,
the love the family members give
to one another sustains them.

In his book *When Bad Things Happen to Good People,* Rabbi Harold S. Kushner points out that when times are at their worst, the love the family members give to one another sustains them. He suggests that the love families offer one another in these times is God's own love, manifest on earth. Many people faced with a life-threatening illness get angry at God for causing their hardship. Kushner argues that God does not cause illness; rather, God is present to comfort people through the love and support of spouse, family, friends, and church.

We personally have not had to face these times of "sickness" as a couple, but we do pray regularly and fervently. We make a special effort not to pray *for* things; instead, we have developed the habit of praying to accept God's will. Although it is so tempting to pray, "God, please make Grandpa's cancer go away," we know that God is not in the business of granting favors like that. Instead, we try to pray, "God, please make us all strong enough to endure Grandpa's illness. Please help us to accept your will and love and to support one another as much as we can."

As Kushner suggests and as the Prayer of Saint Francis describes, we need help in acting as God's instruments, as "means of God's peace." We have seen miraculous feats performed by people whose spouse was gravely ill. These were not instances of sudden healing or anything as dramatic as that. Instead, the miracles we have seen have been simple acts of strength and courage, like a reassuring smile when inside they were terrified or an offer of comfort when inside they were weeping.

People who are in love with each other are capable of incredible acts of bravery that they would not have believed themselves capable of— acts they never would have thought necessary. No marriage partners ever expect the part in the wedding vows about sickness to apply to them, but when they are sick, how lucky married people are to have someone close at hand to manifest God's love!

Sharing the Good Times

To close this chapter, we would like to mention one other thing about good times and bad, sickness and health. If you will be fortunate enough to experience good times and good health in your marriage, you can be certain that others will not. Marriages and families are in trouble everywhere, and plenty of people are sick. All of them need to be assured of God's presence on earth. This reality is an opportunity for happily married couples to share their love with the world.

Do not hoard the gifts
you will give to each other
or those God will bestow on you.

Do not hoard the gifts you will give to each other or those God will bestow on you. Share them with people who need them. Being a good listener for a friend who is having marital difficulties might be just what is needed to help that marriage get past a rough spot. A letter to older or faraway relatives reminds them that they are important to you, even if you cannot see them every day. Visits to those in the hospital, in jail, or in a nursing home remind them that God is alive on earth and working through people.

Of course, married couples are not the only ones who can share their own and God's love with the world, but we think they have a particular responsibility to share their good fortune with others by contributing time, talent, or treasure to some needy cause in a specific way. Spouses can support each other in these gestures of kindness and also teach their children to do the same.

Chapter 4

"I Will Love You and Honor You"

Living God's Greatest Gift

In a Mediterranean port, about two decades after Jesus' Resurrection, a small but growing community of Christians was struggling with the proper way to live their faith. Among the many questions that troubled these people of Corinth, one concerned the appropriate role of marriage in the Christian life. Because these Corinthians, along with other early Christians, expected that Jesus would be returning at any moment, they were not certain that marriage made sense any longer. They were also dealing with a number of other issues, and word got back to the person who had founded their community: Paul, who was in Ephesus at the time.

Paul wrote to assure them of the goodness of marriage and insisted that those who are married should remain so. He also affirmed the importance of celibacy for those who do not marry. The First Letter to the Corinthians has a beautiful and moving passage about love; many modern couples include it in their marriage ceremony:

Love is patient; love is kind; love is not envious or boastful or arrogant or rude. It does not insist on its own way; it is not irritable or resentful; it does not rejoice in wrongdoing, but rejoices in the truth. It bears all things, believes all things, hopes all things, endures all things.

Love never ends. . . . And now faith, hope, and love abide, these three; and the greatest of these is love. (1 Corinthians 13:4–13)

What a powerful description! These words, written nearly two thousand years ago, still speak directly to anyone who has ever experienced love. They are the best working definition of love we have seen. They state what love is: patient, kind; what it is not: envious, boastful, arrogant, rude, selfish, irritable, resentful; and what it does: bears, believes, hopes, endures, and never fails. With all that love has going for it, why are so many people afraid of love?

We have seen countless friends, relatives, and acquaintances of ours come face to face with love and run screaming in terror in the opposite direction. Perhaps not actually screaming in terror, but clearly they were afraid of something. One friend of ours follows this pattern: he shows interest in a woman as long as she remains uninterested in him. As soon as she starts to return his interest, he is no longer attracted. We know a woman who dooms every relationship she enters by going out of her way to find fault with her partner.

"Love is patient; love is kind."

What is it that makes this experience of love so profound and so frightening, causing some to go through incredible feats of emotional gymnastics to avoid being snared? Yet, at the same time, it is what most people desire: a partner, a soul mate. Throughout the ages, writers have extolled and scientists have studied love. Love is the topic of song, poetry, sculpture, painting, and drama. Homage to love generally takes up an inordinate amount of human time and effort.

What Is This Thing Called Love?

To consider love and the role love plays in marriage, look first at the different kinds of love that humans experience. For most of you, the first type of love you encountered is the love you have for your parents. Initially, this is usually a fairly selfish form of love, one from which you benefit without much intentional reciprocation. Eventually you grow to realize that your parents are also on the receiving end of this love relationship, and you begin to love them for their sake as well as for yours.

Children have a remarkable capacity to love their parents unconditionally. We are amazed at how readily our own children forgive us when we screw up as parents, when we are not as patient or as kind as we should be. Our children's love for us is far closer to perfection than our parenting skills could ever be.

Another kind of love is familiar to those of you who have siblings: the love of a brother or a sister is quite different from the love you have for your parents. Sibling love often plays an important role in the development of a person's capacity to love maturely. With your siblings you first experience sharing, competition, cooperation, and other aspects of the relationships you will encounter in adulthood.

A third distinct type of love is the love you have for friends. The love of friendship teaches you something that love of your family members often cannot: love relationships are not always permanent. As children, most people are "trapped" in their relationships with siblings. Despite your bickering with your younger sister or your pestering of your older brother, you cannot leave the relationship, nor can they (at least as children). When it comes right down to it, you really do love them, although you might not want to admit it to them.

This is not the case with friends. You have to deal with a degree of trust, negotiation, and fear of loss with your friends that you typically do not experience with family members. Also, many people achieve with their friends a level of intimacy they do not feel comfortable sharing with family members. Your friends are the first people who require your choice about whether to love them. These aspects of this unique kind of early love will help you to love better later in your life.

> *You must love yourself before you can have a mature love for someone else.*

These three forms of love share some important characteristics. For one, they develop in you the capacity to love others as well as yourself. Most experts (if there is such a thing as an expert on love) agree that you must love yourself before you can have a mature love for someone else. Love relationships with parents, siblings, and friends teach you that you are capable of loving others and that you are lovable.

Sadly, the results do not always work out that way. We know people who were taught in these early relationships that they are not unconditionally worthwhile and lovable, that they are only lovable if they live up to certain standards or behave in certain ways. Sometimes these people are unable to overcome their feelings of self-doubt, even as adults, and so they never experience the joy of genuinely mature love.

Another quality these three forms of love share is that they are not passionate (that is, not sexual). This feature in a love relationship emerges later; people typically experience it for the first time during adolescence.

> *All love relationships display varying degrees of three characteristics: intimacy, commitment, and passion.*

Some scholars who study love (for example, psychologists Robert Sternberg and Elaine Hatfield) say that all love relationships display varying degrees of three characteristics: intimacy, commitment, and passion. Intimacy is the extent to which you share your thoughts and feelings (in short, yourself) with someone and are interested in that person's thoughts and feelings. Commitment is the desire to be together with a person for the long term, to defend, protect, and stand by the loved one. Passion is the degree to which you are physically and emotionally attracted to someone.

A strong friendship, with its love of companionship, has a high degree of commitment and intimacy but little passion. You want to be with your friends, to share with them, and to stand by them, but you do not particularly want to kiss them. On the other hand, passion combined with intimacy but without commitment is likely to result in a brief and intense relationship, an infatuation. Such a relationship flares up and is intense but typically does not last. A more unusual combination is passion and commitment but without intimacy, which may result in a long-term relationship that makes one or both partners feel guarded or distant.

The combination of all three elements—commitment, intimacy, and passion—is a promising recipe for marriage. A couple preparing for marriage should consider each of these three aspects of love separately.

Are You Committed?

More than one confirmed bachelor has pointed out to us that people can apply the word *commitment* equally to entering a long-term relationship or a hospital for the mentally ill. Not surprisingly, we married folk take exception to that comparison. We will agree with this much: it is not good for your mental health to enter a marriage if you do not feel genuinely committed to your partner. Commitment, when used in reference to a marriage relationship, means standing by each other.

When we were first married, a year after we graduated from college, we moved about a thousand miles from our parents, our old community, and most of our friends to attend graduate school. It was difficult for us to be so far away from what was familiar and to start our life together in a different place. As people new to the area, we had few friends or acquaintances. As graduate students, we had very little money. As newlyweds, we were adjusting to life together.

Contrary to popular myth, this adjustment takes more than simply figuring out how to squeeze the toothpaste or remembering to put the seat up or down. This period in our lives was a struggle. At times we were homesick for our friends and family, frustrated with having to do without, or just angry with each other for squeezing the toothpaste the wrong way or leaving the seat up.

It was our commitment to each other that got us through these times. We had promised each other . . . and everyone we knew . . . and God and the church . . . that we two were now committed to each other. This commitment helped tremendously and made us realize that to be happy, we were going to have to put a lot of effort into making this marriage work, and work we did. When we think back on it, that part of our marriage included some of our happiest moments and some of our worst.

Many married couples indicate that the early years of their marriage were like this—characterized by highs and lows (like our stock market analogy in the previous chapter). Virtually all agree that they did not expect this outcome when going into the marriage. This fact accounts for the statistic that most of the marriages that fail do so within the first five or six years. Couples preparing for marriage need to make sure that their level of commitment to each other is strong enough to sustain them through this initial period and through the other challenges we discussed in chapter 3.

Are You Intimate?

Intimacy is another word with more than one meaning. People often use the word *intimate* as the euphemism for sexually active, but here we give it more of an emotional quality: meaning to be very close with each other by sharing what is private or personal. Although two people may be instantly attracted to each other, intimacy almost always takes more time to develop.

Suppose that someone you meet for the first time asks, "How are you?" It is inappropriate to respond, "I've been frustrated because I'm afraid to ask out a person I'm attracted to, because I'm still so hurt from my last relationship." This is way too much information to give to someone you've just met. Might you discuss this with your best friend? Sure, but you don't become best friends with a person without investing some time together. This investment is one of the great benefits of the dating and engagement periods and a reason why couples generally should not rush into marriage. When you get married, you should know each other quite well.

Although two people may be instantly attracted to each other, intimacy almost always takes more time to develop.

We received a wedding invitation a few years ago that had a photograph of the engaged couple as children (they had been neighbors while growing up). Beneath the picture are the words, "Today I get to marry my best friend." How lucky they were to marry someone they knew so well! Intimacy is connection, and most people who have been married a long time indicate that they grow more emotionally intimate with their spouse as time goes by.

It is amazing to watch the communication between two people who have been together for most of their lives. They need not even speak to each other much of the time, and yet they know what the other is thinking. Every couple we know who have been together for any length of time have developed a code that they use to communicate in public—a series of looks, gestures, and shorthand phrases.

For example, we have certain facial expressions we use at parties: the "I'm ready to leave" look, the "please don't tell that story" look, the "please rescue me from this conversation" look, and the "I love you" look, among others. These expressions reflect a degree of intimacy that took time to develop but that now allows us to connect with each other from across a room. Not surprisingly, intimacy and commitment are interconnected; usually, as one grows, so too does the other.

Are You Passionate?

Commitment is about the durability of a relationship; intimacy is about the closeness; passion is about the intensity. Undoubtedly, passion is the aspect of a relationship that is the most exciting, the most exhilarating, and the most intoxicating. Passion moves a relationship from friendship to romance.

Commitment is about the durability of a relationship; intimacy is about the closeness; passion is about the intensity.

Passion is almost universally associated with heat and cold: you burn with passion; you have a flame for someone; the spark or the flame of romance dies out; she turns cold; he has no fire anymore.

Passion, unlike commitment and intimacy, can be almost instantaneous. When some couples refer to love at first sight, they probably do not mean that they experienced an instant desire to share their deepest secrets or that they immediately wanted to spend the rest of their life with someone. They mean that they were instantly attracted to a person.

For other couples, passion grows over time as intimacy and commitment increase. This process can be another benefit of the engagement period. As two people plan their life together and share more of themselves with each other, their feelings of love and attraction are likely to intensify. There is some evidence that men and women differ slightly in this regard: men are more likely to feel an immediate sense of attraction to a particular person, whereas women are more likely to find a potential partner's attractiveness increasing as they get to know the person more deeply. Of course, these generalizations do not apply to everyone in all situations.

Maintaining passion in marriage is a subject of considerable debate. Some argue that passion is important in a successful marriage; others say that it is likely to fade over time and be replaced by comfortable familiarity. Evidence supports both claims. In our case, twelve-plus years of marriage have not reduced the passion we feel for each other; our level of intimacy and commitment continues to grow.

Feelings of fairly intense passion are the norm for engaged couples; the important thing is to discern whether this is the only element of love driving the relationship. Passion is a wonderful and exciting experience, but it can also be distracting and even blind a couple to the possibility that they might not be suitable for each other over the long term. If commitment and intimacy are not present, passion by itself will probably not suffice.

On Our Honor

After you promise in your wedding vows to love your partner (to be committed, intimate, and passionate), you promise as well to honor this special person. What does it mean to honor someone?

*What does it mean
to honor someone?*

Like most of the other key promises in the wedding vows, the word *honor* has several meanings. We use the word to mean to pay tribute to someone, to treat a person fairly and respectfully, and to see a promise through. All of these definitions apply to married life. Couples pay tribute to each other through gratitude and with the kinds of additional actions we described in chapter 2. They treat each other respectfully by living in an equitable relationship. They fulfill their marital promises by remaining committed to each other and living their vows every day.

This notion of living an equitable relationship in a marriage is a tricky one. Critics of marriage argue that marriage is inherently inequitable, benefiting the man more than the woman. Although we certainly recognize that some inequality in marriages does exist, this problem is not a necessary aspect of a marriage. Inequity also exists in many nonmarital relationships. Equity and balance in a marriage are the responsibility of both partners. They have to guard against exploiting and being exploited by the spouse.

We know couples who are very happy distributing responsibilities, such that one person is the primary moneymaker while the other is the primary home manager. In these relationships the responsibilities of housekeeping, child rearing, cooking, and household budgeting are in large part the obligation of just one person. The other partner is in charge of working outside the home to finance the operation.

We also know couples who have determined that the best way for them to live equitably is to divide most tasks about as evenly as they can. In these marriages both husband and wife work outside the home and also prepare meals, do housework, raise the children, take care of finances, and so on. Still other couples, like us, divide the responsibilities depending upon what the job is: child rearing is the responsibility of both, but balancing the checkbook is one person's job, and home repair belongs to the other.

Whether or not couples are "traditional" in their distribution of responsibilities, the most important thing is the extent to which each partner believes that the distribution is fair. Problems are likely to arise when one person thinks that the allocation of responsibility is uneven. People who conclude that they are putting more effort into their relationship than their partner is (anything from emotional investment to household chores) are likely to experience frustration and anger. Those who think their partner is investing more in the relationship than they are will probably experience guilt.

Frustration, anger, and guilt are not conducive to a happy marriage. If they start to experience such feelings, couples ought to discuss these issues, not only during the pre-Cana preparation for marriage but also after the wedding. Simply expressing appreciation for the things each partner does for the relationship (one definition of *honor*) is sometimes enough to restore equity. Other cases require a radical change in behavior.

In our own marriage, we experience both kinds of inequity. Most of the time, a simple conversation initiated by the person who perceives the imbalance is all it takes to resolve the problem. We can easily see the imbalance, once it is pointed out, and we rationally agree on the solution.

The issue gets complicated when we do not see eye to eye on the perceived inequity. When this difficulty sometimes occurs in our marriage, the solution is more elusive. After we talk things out and still cannot come to an agreement on the extent or even the existence of an imbalance in some aspect of our relationship, we have to abandon rationality and appeal to emotions. We simply have to remember how much we love each other, how committed we are to our marriage, and then come up with something to help the situation. Never forget that compromise and adjustment are part of any lasting relationship and that these also have to be shared equitably. If one spouse is doing all the adjusting, the other is not doing enough honoring.

If one spouse is doing all the adjusting, the other is not doing enough honoring.

The purpose of this chapter is to discuss love and honor in marriage. Love, balance, fairness, and adjustment are integral parts of marriage. These are active, not passive, qualities; you must cultivate and nurture them.

One false belief has contributed to many marital difficulties through the years: that marital happiness should just come because you want it to or because you are told to expect it. An old Irish expression says, "Never pray for potatoes without a hoe in your hand." You must be willing to work for the things you want. Because marital happiness is well worth having, it is worth putting some effort into it. Love will provide you with the motivation to put forth the effort; honor will guide you in how you direct that effort.

Chapter 5

"All the Days of My Life"

When Husband and Wife Become Father and Mother

In the introduction of this book, we pointed out that being married is like breathing: something you do every day of your life from the day you exchange vows. In the chapters leading up to this one, we have tried to show how a couple can live each of the vows every day.

In this last chapter, we will look at the other major life vocation that often emerges from marriage: parenting. Remember also from the wedding vows that one of the preconditions for two young and healthy people to marry in the church is that they will accept children lovingly from God and raise them according to the laws of the church.

We postponed the discussion of parenting until this final chapter because we were afraid that if we had not waited, parenting would have dominated the entire book; the topic is that big. Don't forget that we are the parents of young children: a particularly prominent part of who we are at this point in our life and in our marriage.

Becoming a parent—as profound a life change as becoming a married person, if not more so—brings a whole new set of responsibilities and adjustments to go along with new kinds of experiences of joy, love, and pride. Clearly, your vows extend to your family when you have children. If you are untrue to your spouse, you also betray your children, who share good times and bad, sickness and health. In short, when you have children, you invite them into your life and extend your promises of love and fidelity to them.

We do not intend this chapter to be a how-to guide for parenting. First, plenty of those are already out there, and second, even though we try hard to be excellent parents, we are not good enough at it to tell others how to do it. Instead, we want to describe how parenthood impacts a marital relationship and leads a couple to a greater understanding of the significance of their marriage.

At Mass recently, on Pro-Life Sunday, our parish priest gave a homily on the gift of children. He began with a simple equation, $1 + 1 + 1 = 1$, to show that the love of one woman plus the love of one man plus the love of God equals one child.

A children's story begins by describing how a man and a woman loved each other so much that they got married and had a child so that their love could walk around in the world. What a beautiful way to describe a child! Of course, the author probably did not write this while changing a stinky diaper at four in the morning or dealing with a three-year-old's temper tantrum.

> *Becoming a parent is as profound a life change as becoming a married person.*

Children are miraculous, beautiful, and innocent little humans capable of incredible acts of love and kindness. They are also irrational, stubborn, and needy little twerps adept at performing unbelievable acts of mischief and deception. This is the parenting scene: the whole behavioral and emotional package—the good, the bad, and the ugly. Children take up an amazing amount of their parents' time and energy, making it even more important that the parents spend time conscientiously being a spouse each day.

Children are miraculous, beautiful, and innocent little humans capable of incredible acts of love and kindness.

Pregnancy

When we first learned we were expecting a child, we felt an interesting blend of excitement and dread. On the one hand, we had prayed for a child for a long time and were very grateful finally to be expecting one. On the other hand, we were extremely nervous about the responsibility of parenting. We were not sure we were capable of even keeping a baby alive, let alone raising one to be a decent human being. This is to say nothing of the fear we had about the risks of pregnancy and childbirth.

There was also the concern we both felt about how the new arrival would affect our marriage. We had grown accustomed to being a couple, spending our free time the way we wanted, and frankly, not sharing each other with anyone else in a serious way. What was this third, albeit small, person going to demand of us in time and energy? How would being a parent change our marriage?

In an effort to ease ourselves into this transition, we hit upon the brilliant idea of getting a dog—a beagle puppy, to be exact. We figured a dog would give us practice at keeping another living thing alive. Pet training seemed sort of like parenting. Well, as we write this, Bill the Beagle is still with us, so we accomplished our goal of keeping him alive, plus we had to train him, and we give him affection that he returns exponentially. Thinking that pet ownership would prepare us for parenting was a mistake only a nonparent could make. We found out, to no one's surprise, that children are much more complex than dogs.

Our pregnancies have been highlights of our marriage.

The puppy notwithstanding, our pregnancies have been highlights of our marriage. They have been times of preparation, in some ways not unlike our engagement. We had to organize our living arrangements again; our families were excited and even threw a shower or two, and we reveled in the time we got to spend together just imagining what the future would be like for us.

So that we would know what was happening and when, we made it a point for *both* of us to go to all of the prenatal examinations during the first pregnancy. We attended birth-preparation classes to get us ready for the labor and the delivery. We had fun decorating the nursery together. In short, we took the opportunity to learn and grow together as we prepared for the next phase of our marriage.

Childbirth

The experience of childbirth itself had a significant impact on our marriage. Our first child was born a few weeks before his due date. We reached the hospital just forty minutes before he arrived in our life. Our second and third were born at a more relaxed pace and in a peaceful atmosphere.

The birth of a child is like no other experience in life for either the mother or the father. We are very glad that the father who is present for the delivery has replaced the stereotype of the husband who paces around the waiting room while his wife delivers their child. The father has been elevated to the title of "coach" in the birthing process, but this is an exaggerated term, at least in our case. A more accurate descriptor would be somewhere between spectator and cheerleader. Even so, the births of our children were three special moments—each one unique— that we look back on with fondness.

The birth of a child
is like no other experience in life
for either the mother or the father.

Granted, our birthing experiences are not for everyone. We used a nurse-midwife and tried to keep the process chemical free and as natural as possible, with both of us together for the entire time. Some couples exclude the father from the delivery room, want only a physician to deliver the baby, and choose to manage the pain of labor with anesthesia. Like us, other parents want to maintain a high degree of control over the process: who will be welcome in the delivery room, who will hold the baby first and for how long, when the baby will be cleaned and weighed, and so on. Still others take comfort in handing over these decisions to someone else, allowing the parents to concentrate on the important business at hand.

The critical issue here, we think, is that both husband and wife use the pregnancy as an opportunity to discuss childbirth and are happy with the kind of childbirth experience they have chosen (if they are lucky enough to have choices; some high-risk pregnancies preclude certain childbirth options).

Our childbirth experiences were very special for us, more so because we shared them. We are grateful that we can *both* look back with a sense of wonder, awe, joy, and fondness at these sacred events.

Parenting

Bearing children turned out to have a profound impact on our marriage but not in the ways we anticipated. We expected to love our children, and we do. What we did not realize is that sharing our love with our children would not detract or divert our love for each other. It is like those old Doritos ads: "Eat all you want; we'll make more."

Love does not obey the laws
of conservation.

When the gift of a child came our way, we continued to love each other just as much as we always had, yet we found that we had more love to give to our child. When we had our second baby, the same thing happened, as it did with our third. Love, apparently, does not obey the laws of conservation; we simply produced more of it when we had more children. This has been one of the most pleasant surprises of bringing children into the world.

Time, however, is one thing we cannot simply produce more of. It would be nice if the birth of each child included two or three additional hours per day for the parents, allowing them to invest in their own relationship each day without depriving their child of anything necessary. Sad to say, couples only get the same twenty-four hours, regardless of how many children they have. When a child is very young, twenty-four hours is simply not enough time. It's an unfair situation, but there you are.

You can usually tell new parents in a crowd: they have circles under their eyes and smell of baby powder. Babies have strange sleep schedules, by which we mean that they do not sleep and wake up like adults do. Nighttime has little meaning to them. Babies have two times: happy time and unhappy time. They spend much of their happy time sleeping and almost all of their unhappy time awake.

What makes them unhappy? To most new parents, it appears to be sleeping parents. Babies seem to have a tiny internal alarm clock that goes off and wakes them up whenever mom and dad start to doze off. In reality this reaction probably has more to do with hunger. Babies have little stomachs, so they need to eat often. Parents love their child, so they adjust their own schedule to that of their baby and end up with circles under their eyes.

All this sleeplessness takes its toll on a marital relationship and makes parents grouchy; at least it did in our case. Grouchiness tends not to be real good for a marriage. This was the time we had to remind ourselves how lucky we are to have each other to share this experience, how lucky we are to have a healthy baby, and how short this period of our life is when it comes right down to it. Before we knew it, the baby was sleeping through the night, eating solid foods, walking, and then going to school.

As children grow,
new challenges
confront their parents.

As children grow, new challenges confront their parents. For too many couples, parenting becomes a wedge in their marriage, driving them apart rather than bonding them together. Disagreements about child rearing are a significant source of marital stress. Like every other conflict, these disagreements can be minimized if they are discussed in advance. Will your children receive an allowance? What time will be bedtime? Will you use corporal punishment with your children? If so, under what circumstances? If not, what techniques will you use to influence their behavior? It is *very* important for parents to agree on these matters, particularly on issues about responding to a child's wrongdoing.

The problem with trying to prepare for parenting is that you cannot possibly anticipate every situation you will face that requires a decision, for example, what the appropriate course of action is when a child does thus and so. Facing these unanticipated predicaments puts a marriage to the test.

We think it is important that parents have some good rules of thumb to guide them through these uncertain times. In our case we follow several rules. First, we have agreed as parents that we are, as much as possible, a parenting unit. We try to avoid disagreeing in front of our children about on-the-spot parenting decisions.

If one of us disagrees with the other's response to a situation, so our rule goes, we are to discuss it privately and make alternative suggestions rather than simply step in and defend the child or countermand the decision. This approach keeps our children from trying to play off one of us against the other, at least in theory. Of course, we do not execute this plan flawlessly, but we keep trying. For the most part, it works; our children have had little success in finagling a late afternoon snack out of dad when mom has already said no.

A second rule we have agreed to is that we are both empowered to discipline, praise, and show affection to our children. We know many families where the father is in charge of doling out the discipline, but all the hugs and kisses come from mom. We do not think this is fair to fathers. There is no "Wait until your father gets home!" in our house.

Third, we try to let natural consequences drive the appropriate outcome of our children's behavior. For example, we make our children wear seat belts because the natural consequences of their not doing so would be too dire. When we cannot follow this policy of natural consequences, we try to be matter-of-fact rather than angry when enforcing a rule (again, easier said than done).

Having these rules to guide us has not prevented all disagreements about child rearing but has caused us to be conscientious about our parenting decisions and respectful of each other when these judgments need to be made.

Taking Time

In becoming parents, we have never forgotten that we are partners in both parenthood and marriage. Sometimes the demands of parenthood can be so great that we neglect each other as marriage partners, which is easy to do as our children grow older and their life, as well as ours, get busier.

We know families whose existence has become more or less enslaved by the social, musical, and athletic schedules of their children. Some parents see no falling off in the quality of their marital relationship, but others complain that their marriage is not as fun, romantic, and passionate as it used to be. Most of these folks never decided that their children's schedules would dominate them; it just happened.

To avoid being overwhelmed, parents should build in some time for themselves as well as for the entire family when they plan the upcoming seasons. We make a point of going out together, just the two of us, at least a couple of times a month. For some years we even enjoyed a weekly night out together because we had enrolled in a ballroom dancing class with friends. We talk to each other on the phone daily, just to say hi. We also make a point of doing family activities—a trip to a museum, a visit to relatives, a bike ride—a few times a month. For us it is also important to eat dinner together every day and to attend Sunday Mass as a family.

These activities are needed for balance. We know that they will be harder to maintain as our children grow older and their interests expand. But we are committed to being mindful of our needs as a couple and a family as we develop our individual interests.

Finally, when we fill our calendar, we make sure it is with things that are fulfilling: for instance, learning experiences, memorable occasions, and commitments that will be enjoyable or will contribute to our personal and professional growth. Although not every experience must be significant or meaningful, we try to consider the most worthwhile ways to use the hours given to us. We make sure to leave open enough spots on our schedules for spontaneous opportunities and simply resting. Creating a sense of organization, balance, and meaning in our life has always been important to us, both individually and as a family.

Conclusion

Partners for Life

"I take you to be my spouse. I promise to be true to you in good times and in bad, in sickness and in health. I will love you and honor you all the days of my life. I will do all these things all the days of my life." (Adapted from the *Rite of Marriage*)

Since the introduction of this book, when we first looked at the matrimonial vows in the Catholic Rite of Marriage, we have tried to write about our marriage and the marriages of people we know. As we look back at what we have written, the only thing we know for sure is that we have not been completely successful in conveying what our own marriage is really like. We have left out a lot of details, some intentionally, some accidentally. We fight, we make up, we forgive, we celebrate, we take pride, we pout, we laugh, we cherish, we grow, we forget, we forgive again. In short, we live. Much of what we have omitted we have done simply because our writing is not good enough to capture fully the emotional experiences that our marriage has entailed. We take comfort in the knowledge that if you are in love with someone who is in love with you, you probably have a good idea of what we mean.

As we write this book, we have been married for about 4,500 days—a little over twelve years. At the beginning of our marriage, that number would have seemed incomprehensibly large to us. Looking back, we do not see it as being that long. We do not know with certainty what the next 4,500 days or the 4,500 after that hold for our marriage. We do know that no matter how many days we are given on earth, we will spend each one of them living our wedding vows, which continue to bind and guide us.

Living our vows does make us confident
that we will continue to have faith
in each other and in our marriage.

Living our vows will not guarantee that every day will be happy, that we will remain free of illness or financial difficulty, or that things will always work out as we hope they will. But living our vows does make us confident that we will continue to have faith in each other and in our marriage. Faith gives us strength; strength in turn gives us faith.

The special thing about marriage is that we do not live it in twelve-year chunks; we live it daily. We patiently spend each day being true to each other, in good times and in bad, in sickness and in health. We love and honor each other, and every once in a while, we note that a significant amount of time has gone by. On these occasions, which are usually holidays or anniversaries, we take time to stop and say to each other, "Thanks for being my partner in all of this."

We hope that by reading this book, you have gained from our experiences some insights that will help you prepare for and live your own marriage. We know, however, that the most meaningful and lasting insights come from your own experience. You can only study and prepare so much for marriage. There comes a time when more reading about it, more engagement counseling, and more research produce no greater readiness.

There will always be an element of faith in *getting* married, just as there is always an element of faith in *being* married. You can never be absolutely certain in advance that you have chosen the right person or that the time is right. Perhaps this uncertainty is part of God's plan for marriage: that it is based on an act of faith. You must believe in yourself; you must believe in your partner. In so doing, you practice being both a faithful and a faith-filled person. The great thing about *this* act of faith is that you have someone's hand to hold as you take that deep breath— and leap.

For Further Reading

Finley, Kathleen. *The Seeker's Guide to Building a Christian Marriage: Eleven Essential Skills.* Chicago: Loyola Press, 2000.

Hart, Thomas H., and Kathleen R. Fischer. *Promises to Keep: Developing the Skills of Marriage.* Mahwah, NJ: Paulist Press, 1991.

John Paul II, Pope. *The Theology of the Body: Human Love in the Divine Plan.* Boston: Pauline Books and Media, 1997.

Kehrwald, Leif. *Marriage and the Spirituality of Intimacy.* Cincinnati, OH: St. Anthony Messenger Press, 1996.

McDonald, Patrick J., and Claudette M. McDonald. *The Soul of Marriage.* Mahwah, NJ: Paulist Press, 1995.

Thomas, David M., and John L. Thomas. *Beginning Your Marriage.* Chicago: ACTA Publications, 1994.

Acknowledgments *(continued from page 4)*